Planning a Training Strategy

The Competent Trainer's Toolkit Series
by David G. Reay

This book is the second 'tool' in *The Competent Trainer's Toolkit Series*.

The first — *Understanding the Training Function* — stands outside the training cycle. The rest, including this one, deal with the cycle stage by stage, from planning your initial strategy to evaluating the contribution that training makes to the prosperity of your organization.

All these books can be used on training courses or as aids to self development.

Planning a Training Strategy

DAVID G REAY

Kogan Page Ltd, London
Nichols Publishing Company,
New Jersey

Published in association with **OTSU** LIMITED

First published in 1994
Reprinted 1995

Apart from any fair dealing for the purposes of research or private study, or criticism
or review, as permitted under the Copyright, Designs and Patents Act, 1988, this
publication may only be reproduced, stored or transmitted, in any form or by any
means, with the prior permission in writing of the publishers, or in the case of
reprographic reproduction in accordance with the terms of licences issued by the
Copyright Licensing Agency. Enquiries concerning reproduction outside those terms
should be sent to the publishers at the undermentioned address:

Kogan Page Limited
120 Pentonville Road
London N1 9JN

© OTSU Ltd, 1994

Published in the United States of America by Nichols Publishing,
PO Box 6036, East Brunswick, New Jersey 08816

British Library Cataloguing in Publication Data

A CIP record for this book is available from the British Library.

ISBN (UK) 0 7494 1283 6
ISBN (US) 0-89397-429-3

Printed and bound in Great Britain by
Biddles Ltd, Guildford and King's Lynn

Contents

Acknowledgements

This series is to a large extent based on OTSU's experiences during the past decade. Because of this, so many people have been involved in its formulation, it would be impossible to name them all. However, there are a number of people without whose help this series would not have seen the light of day.

I would like therefore to give my sincere thanks to Paul Leach for his constant support with writing, Adrian Spooner for his editing skill, Aidan Lynn for setting the series in motion, Jill Sharpe and Kathleen Gibson for design and desk-top publishing, Dorothy Reay and Amanda Froggatt for proof-reading and finally Dolores Black at Kogan Page who didn't mind flexible deadlines.

Introduction

Until quite recently, the target for this book would have been simple to define: 'training manager' would have done the trick very succinctly.

Nowadays, however, an increasing number of people within an organization recognize that they have an important role to play in training — if not as full-time dedicated trainers, then as committed supporters of the training function. For example, there are line managers who may be asked to guide members of their team through specific modules, or to identify which members of their team need which training and when. There are also directors of businesses who may be asked not only to support (and pay for!) individual training initiatives, but also a whole training strategy.

As the contribution which people make to the success of an organization is seen to grow in importance, so more people need to be aware of what training strategy is all about: what it involves, what needs to be considered, what its costs and benefits are. Consequently, this book is for anyone who has an interest in or a potential contribution to make to an organization's training strategy.

Of course, I expect that dedicated trainers and training managers will find this book an invaluable help as they get on with the task of planning a training strategy. Without an effective strategy the training function will be seen at best as rudderless, at worst as positively dangerous. This is unacceptable. Training has the power to unlock enormous reserves of potential in an organization's people. It is a vital part of every trainer's task to ensure that this potential is released in a way which provides optimum benefits for both the organization and its people.

To achieve such a release of potential requires strategic thinking.

So What is Planning a Training Strategy All About?

Given that the training function has an important role to play in any organization, your strategy as a trainer must aim to maximize the benefits.

In its broadest terms, your strategy will follow two lines, a 'political' line and a 'practical' one. Your political strategy will aim to ensure that the training function has the correct profile within the organization. If you have too low a profile, your opinion will not be sought about matters which concern you directly, and which you could influence to everyone's benefit, until it is too late. Training is an afterthought in these situations, and the only 'strategy' available to you is to do what people want; which may not be what they need.

It's possible that your function has too high a profile, and people feel unable to take even the smallest initiative without first checking with you. This situation is likely to restrict your organization's opportunities for growth and improvement.

So there is a need to establish the training function's position within the order of things in a way which enables it to have maximum effect.

Next comes your 'practical' strategy. At this stage you will need to consider training needs and priorities, as well as the merits and demerits of different training methodologies, and resourcing in terms of time, people and money. Even here, though, purely instructional considerations are not enough; there are other issues, such as the business culture, to consider.

So much for what a training strategy **is**; planning that strategy will involve a detailed scheme of information gathering and response.

Objectives

By the time you have completed this book, you will be able to:

- identify the business needs of an organization and their training implications
- categorize the people who use training and analyse their perception of the service they receive
- identify the training methodology not only available but also acceptable to the organization
- analyse the organization itself, and
- decide the resources necessary to provide an effective training function within it.

Training and Development Lead Body Competences

Many trainers and training managers in the UK are actively seeking professional vocational qualifications, through the National Vocational Qualification route. There are competences at level 3 and level 4 of the NVQ in Training and Development for which you will be able to use this book as part of your portfolio of evidence.

I have prepared, on the following page, a matrix which matches a list of assignments in this book and the competences, published in autumn 1994, which appear in the scheme booklets provided by the awarding bodies. Simply tick off the numbered assignments as you do them. Then, when you've completed this book, you can include the book itself together with any supporting documents you may create as you work through it in your NVQ portfolio. This simple matching technique will allow your NVQ assessor easily to locate your evidence and match it against the relevant criteria. Each assignment goes towards meeting performance criteria outlined in the elements shown.

MCI Unit 9

Assignment on Pages	The Assignment Counts as Evidence Towards these Elements					
21	B111	E212	E213			
25	MCI Unit 9					
31	B111	B121	E212	E213		
36	E212	E213				
48	B111	B112				
52	MCI Unit 8					
60	A122	A123	A131	A132		
63	A124					
69	B112	B121	B211			
75	E111	E121	E123	E212	B213	
92	B111	B112	B122	B123	B211	E121

A122   Identify the potential contribution of training and development to organizational development
A123   Determine organizations and objectives for training and development
A124   Gain commitment for the contribution of training and development to an organization
A131   Collect information for an organization's training and development needs analysis
A132   Analyse information on organizational training and development needs
B111   Identify potential strategies for training and development in an organization
B112   Devise a strategy for training and development within an organization
B121   Select options for implementing training and development objectives
B122   Develop a training and development implementation plan
B123   Prepare the implementation of the plan
B211   Select options for meeting learning requirements
E111   Specify processes for evaluating the contribution of training and development to an organization
E121   Identify potential improvement to training and development within an organization
E122   Plan the introduction of improvements to training and development within an organization
E212   Collect information to evaluate training and development programmes
E213   Analyse information to improve training and development programmes
MCI Unit 8   Seek, evaluate and organize information for action
MCI Unit 9   Exchange information to solve problems and make decisions

Overview

To help you find your way round this book, we've prepared an overview so that you can see what is contained in each chapter.

Chapter 1 — Business Needs and Training Needs

You will see that by gaining a reputation for realism and pragmatism the training function can play a full part in the strategic planning of the organization as a whole. We explain the benefits of getting the training function into this position of 'influencer'.

Chapter 2 — Sponsors/Customers/Consumers and their Perceptions of Training

This chapter looks at ways in which you can enhance the standing of the training function in the eyes of the people who really matter — by providing them with what they need in the most practical way.

Chapter 3 — Types of Organization

You will examine in some detail five common types of organization, and consider in each case the type of strategy which would be most appropriate. You will look at the features of strategies which have been proved successful in different types of organization.

Chapter 4 — Training Methodology

You can see several practical steps which you can take to keep yourself and your colleagues up-to-date with what is going on in the training world. And you'll examine the criteria you should use to assess whether your new ideas would or would not be successful in your organization.

Chapter 5 — Objectives and Priorities

In this chapter you will see how a well balanced set of training objectives and priorities will take into account the differing requirements of your organization's need for fundamental training, new initiatives, your need to get the correct profile for training in your organization and your need to develop your own personal skills.

It is at this stage that you will meet the 'strategy grid', a tool you will be able to use as you plan your strategy.

Chapter 6 — Strategies and Resources

In this chapter you will see the importance of a training policy statement, and a look at the key elements which should be in it. You'll see as well how action plans relate to the overall strategy document.

There is a section to help you identify the sort of person you need to have in your training team.

We cover the need for a regular formal review of training as an important plank of your policy.

Lastly you consider ways in which you can analyse your current — and expected — use of resources.

Study Advice

This is not a text which you will read once and then put away never to read again, at least I hope not. Its inclusion in the Competent Trainer's Toolkit series indicates that it is designed for you to use in your work as a trainer.

How you work through the book is really up to you. You may, if you wish, work through the pages in order from front to back and cover the whole text in that way. The book is constructed logically so that you can work right through it. Alternatively, you can dip into a chapter at a time, as and when you need to.

There is a range of activities and assignments for me to complete inside each chapter. Activities are distinguished by the fact that there is some feedback — not always in the form of right or wrong answers, because there are not always hard-and-fast right or wrong answers to be had.

Assignments, on the other hand, are an opportunity for you to get out into your organization and ask some of the questions which will help you to analyse your own situation, your own needs. It would be misleading of me to include any 'answers' although I have included comments from my own organization's experiences where appropriate. However, your situation is bound to have its unique features.

As an additional benefit, by completing activities and assignments you will be able to create a body of evidence for your vocational qualification. We suggested earlier that you should keep this text as a record of your study, along with the outcomes of the activities and assignments. Because the book calls on you to write your **own** thoughts and think about your **own** situation it will become your personal record and guide to your understanding of the training function.

You should feel free to write notes at any point in the margins or on the text. In fact, the more notes you write, the more useful this book will be to you in the long term.

Chapter 1

Business Needs and Training Needs

If, as trainers, we want to have credibility, we must emphasize the pragmatic and show how training is tuned-in to the real world of the organization it serves. It is far too easy to adopt the latest buzz words and terms and make spurious comments about what should be happening in the workplace. There are, indeed organizations which have pre-set 'training days' — when personnel 'get trained' whether they need it or not!

The fact is, being tuned-in means understanding exactly what is going on around you. What are the interdependencies between functions — what is working and what is not working — and that means asking a lot of practical, sometimes awkward questions.

Naturally, asking lots of questions will generate a lot of information. But what are you supposed to do with all this information? You might know the overall strategy of the business, the financial state of your organization; its marketing strategy, its operational plan and the future shape of its workforce. So what? How can you put that information to good use?

Most organizational strategies contain an element of enabling people to operate in a way which helps to save time, money and effort, but at the same time maintain, but preferably improve, the quality they provide to their customers.

Take a few moments to think how effective training can make a positive contribution to saving time, money and effort.

- Saving time?

- Saving money?

- Saving effort?

When we tried out this unit with trainers we got a variety of answers. The comments I've given here summarize the main points. You may have others to add.

- **Effective trainers save time** by ensuring that skilled and competent staff are on hand when they are needed, rather than untrained staff who will take longer to do the job and require time to be spent later on rectification.

- **Effective training saves money** by avoiding the untold number of errors which can result from the efforts of untrained staff.

- **Effective training saves effort** by showing people the most effective ways to do things and getting it right first time, rather than having them get it wrong six times first.

So, effective training has a very practical contribution to make to achieving the organization's strategy. Indeed, it could, and should, be argued that any planning process that has not had input from training will necessarily be incomplete. **In fact, the likelihood of the achievement of the strategy is increased the more the training function has input**. (We'll leave the exploration of what constitutes **effective** training until later.)

Here is an example drawn from one of our past experiences.

Case Study

An organization's business plan had identified the launch of a new product in the next year. Training had not been involved in the planning process, so when the training department representative asked these questions there were some very red faces on the planning committee:

- who will install the machinery?
- who will operate the machinery?
- how much will it cost to employ these people?
- how will the people be trained?
- how long will the training and installation take?
- what effect will the change have on the rest of the workplace?

There was no answer readily available. When the representative went on to ask what would happen if the people operating the new machinery and systems were **not** fully trained before start up, other people round the table started to get worried. And rightly so. This kind of situation is not as rare as you might think.

Another area which all organizations seem to be facing to a greater or lesser degree at present is change. This process often involves a strategic, planned approach and the planning process is often carried out with a training input.

The kinds of change I'm thinking of include, among others, things like:

- a move into new markets
- adoption of new technologies
- recruitment of new staff
- shedding existing staff
- a physical move to a new site
- being at one end or the other of a takeover.

Look through the list and make a few notes on why it should be a priority for training to get involved in change situations. See if you can come up with a couple of reasons.

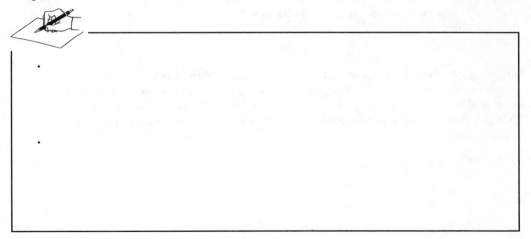

We identified three major reasons why it might be a priority for training to get involved in change situations; you could well have thought of others.

First, **change, by definition, means confronting people with the new**. Without training, the transition to the new could be bloody, brutal and long. But training can provide the knowledge and skills to face up to new responsibilities, working practices and operating systems within a changed working environment quickly and with good will.

Second, **change is frightening**. The right kind of training can help people face their fears in a safe environment. It can help people share fears with their colleagues and can also provide the skills and techniques to help handle change in a positive and beneficial way. People can be encouraged to let go of the old and begin to embrace the new, with less fear of the unknown.

Third, **change is always the focus of attention**. If you want to be noticed as a shaper of your organization's destiny, you need to be contributing to successful change.

Appropriate and successful training can greatly ease the process of change not only for those who are experiencing it, but also for those whose responsibility it is to make sure change occurs. It can, effectively, be an investment in the credibility of the training function.

Training can provide practical guidance and support and also act in the planning phase to remind people that whatever plans are made, and however they are made, they will have some kind of impact on the people involved. The right kind of planned training support can ensure that the impact is both individually and corporately positive.

Summary

In the first chapter you have seen that:

- to be credible, the training function must put emphasis on being pragmatic
- training has a major contribution to make to the planning process
- the training input will impact on people and save time in the implementation of plans
- training will also allow plans to be implemented with less expense and less effort
- training is an essential element in any change scenario.

Chapter 2

Sponsors/Customers/ Consumers and their Perceptions of Training

If training has got a poor reputation now, pretty drastic action will be needed to make it effective in the future. That means that the objectives you set for the training function will depend to a large extent on the current reputation of the function.

Realistically, though, if people have a poor opinion of training, it is unreasonable to ask them to believe in an overnight transformation. Only in fairytales do pumpkins turn into golden coaches and even then you need a fairy godmother.

Let's consider the perceptions which different groups of people have of training. I'll suggest some perceptions which ideally they should have and explore some strategies to help bridge the gap between one and the other. I'll start with sponsors.

Sponsors

By 'sponsors' we mean the senior members of your organization who control, amongst other things, the purse strings. They probably make up a board of some sort: of directors, of governors, of trustees. In a professionally-managed organization, their prime objective will be to ensure that investment in all its forms is concentrated in those areas which will provide the greatest short-term and long-term benefit.

Assignment

So what do the sponsors in your organization think of training? Do you have any way of finding out? Ideally you should talk to them and ask them. However, if there's no formal approach you can take you'll have to start gathering evidence informally. Find written sources of information and talk to people who know. You might find it useful to consider these questions:

- *has funding for training been increasing, static or declining in the last three years?*

- *if money has been generally tight, has training done better, or worse, than other service functions?*

- *how is training staffed?*

- *is training an essential step in a high-flyer's career or a parking-lot for the operationally feeble?*

- *does training get a mention in the annual report? What does it say?*

- *how often does training get a visit from a board member? What questions do they ask? Are they polite or interested?*

- *is training involved in trouble-shooting at times of crisis?*

- *is training asked to contribute at times of expansion?*

If your answers to these questions suggest that training is seen as occupying a backwater in the organization, you need to make a strategic personal choice between accepting the view that training is largely irrelevant, and fighting for a higher profile.

If you decide to fight it, or alternatively if training is already seen as central to the progress of the organization and you want to keep it there, you need to take action. Again, be hard-headed. Good intentions are fine, but they don't deliver a message like qualified information, facts or figures. So, to help you make your case, here are some issues you might like to consider.

1. Make Training Measurable

Find some relevant numbers you can quote to show the contribution training is making to organizational performance.

Can you think of ways of measuring training?

•

•

When I ask trainers to do this exercise at workshops they often come up with items like:

- trainees processed
- logs of training provided
- packages issued or completed.

However, when I ask which is the measure which gives the best idea of the quality of training the answers tend to centre on one word: achievement.

The idea of achievement leads directly to some useful specific ideas. If you can demonstrate some kind of achievement: examinations passed, apprenticeships completed, standards of performance, competences required to achieve the business aims, then the chances are that your board members will regard them as significant. If such figures exist, quote them. If they don't, introduce them as a yardstick of your own performance.

NVQs and SVQs are becoming increasingly popular, as they are visible, incontestable signs of proof that people's level of competence is rising.

2. Make Training Relevant

You've heard about the stewards on the Titanic, rearranging the deckchairs as the ship went down? It may have been in their job descriptions but it was a stupendously irrelevant activity at the time. Training must not be seen as a 'deckchair' activity. Training must be linked to the achievement of the organization's objectives and the objectives of people within the organization. So you need to be aware, not only of the strategic decisions which we talked about in Chapter 1, but also the current main concerns of the organization. The action of the training function must be to develop a strategy for training which is closely linked to these objectives; this is a diplomatic way of giving training a high profile.

Case Study

A prestigious manufacturer of aircraft undercarriages was seeking to diversify its product base and gain access to new customers and new markets. There was an ailing producer of hydraulic equipment in the locality, so the board of the undercarriage manufacturers decided to launch a bid for the hydraulics company. The board also took the opportunity to close down their outdated and oversized production plant and move the two existing businesses on to one modern site.

The training department saw straight away the enormous training needs that this situation generated in the way of:

- practical changes
- cultural changes
- attitude changes

and produced an effective and accurately targeted programme of training initiatives, which was ready to roll two months before the physical move. Because of this, the training manager's position on the strategy team was not only vindicated but greatly strengthened.

3. Tell People What You're Doing

If you want to raise the profile and impact of the training function then you can't afford to sit around waiting for someone to notice what you're doing.

Nobody who matters will come enquiring after the health of the training function if the training function does nothing to make itself visible.

So what do you do?

There are all sorts of ways to do this:

- have you something newsworthy to go into a staff newspaper? Make sure it gets in

- have you done anything novel enough to be worth national or specialist press coverage? Make sure you get the coverage

- could you mount special events, exhibitions, or open days, to which senior management could be invited? Do it

- is there an annual review of training, at which board members are told what the training function has done in the last year and how well or badly? If not carry out a review and give a board member the results.

Remember that people attending such a review will feel a sense of ownership and responsibility. It's a powerful way of developing allies.

Assignment:

1. *From the paragraph above, identify those publicity initiatives which your training function has tried over the last two years.*

2. *Note down any successes — because it is easier to repeat a successful method than attempt a new one.*

3. *Make a list of any achievements or plans that you would like to publicize.*

4. *Match your list of items to publicize:*
   - *first, with the list of your tried initiatives*
   - *second, with the list of initiatives in the paragraph above.*

   Remember to consider:
   - *how many people you want to reach*
   - *who these people are*
   - *exactly what you want to tell them.*

5. *Plan a publicity campaign with*
   - *launch dates*
   - *targets agreed*
   - *end dates*
   - *reviews.*

Customers

It is arguable that everyone who benefits in some way from the service provided by the training function is a 'customer'.

'Customer' in this broad sense would include everyone connected with the organization or who stands to benefit from its survival and prosperity.

For the purposes of planning your strategy, it is more useful to think of your customers as the managers who actually 'buy' your training. These are the people who have the power to say yes or no to your training. These are the people who have the power to spend their training budget with you — or with somebody else — or not at all.

These customers are, in many organizations, able to exercise a good deal of control over how and where they obtain their training, so you should consider them and their needs very carefully.

What are the various alternatives to which customers in your organization could potentially turn to source the training they need for their staff? Write the possibilities here.

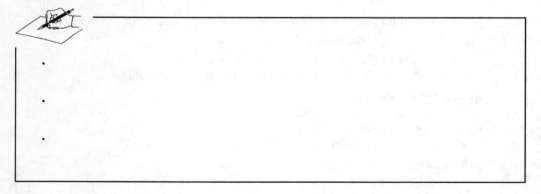

In general terms there are usually three principal choices which can be made. Many customers may adopt a combination of two, or even all three of them, depending on the target groups and their particular training needs.

The three principal choices are to:

- use your in-house service
- go to external suppliers
- do without the training.

Let's look at each more closely.

Customers' First Choice

The first choice is simply to use your in-house service. If that is a conscious decision taken after evaluating all other alternatives, then clearly the training function is well-known and respected. In that case congratulations. You've obviously got a very strong base on which to build.

But it could be simply that your customers are the managers who don't think training is very important, so can't be bothered to look further than the in-house service. If the potential customers who value training are taking the second alternative, your in-house service is providing no more than a crutch to those who are too lazy to stand on their own two feet.

Customers' Second Choice

The second choice is to go to one or more external suppliers. Whether these are providers of public courses, business schools, independent consultants, computer-based training programmers or open learning authors, the fact that customers who might be shopping at your stall are spending their money outside should be causing alarm bells to ring. Once again, though, you need to think things through a little more deeply.

Under what circumstances would you expect, and welcome, the use of external training providers by your customers?

Jot a couple of ideas here.

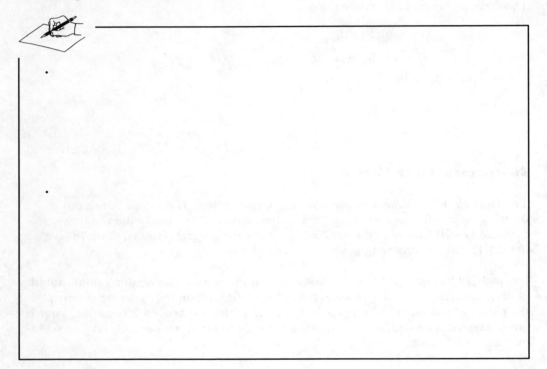

We thought of three sets of circumstances where we'd be quite happy for this to happen.

- We thought first of situations where you have a small group of specialist, technical staff. They may be systems analysts, organization and method people, accountants or programmers. Clearly it would be daft to design an in-house course or training package for just two people a year. It would be far more cost-effective, and the training would be much more reliable and up-to-date, to use an outside provider.

- Second, we thought of people who could benefit from designing and extending their knowledge beyond anything available in-house. We wouldn't expect you to have, for example, an internationally-recognized specialist in market strategy on your team, but there are several business schools in Europe and America which do.

- Finally, we thought of members of staff who need a fresh outlook on their job, as much as any particular training. For somebody in this situation, who has maybe been around a long time and no longer sees any challenge or new approaches to the job, the opportunity to meet some different people from other organizations and discuss some new ideas could provide just the lift needed.

So there are circumstances when external training can be beneficial. But you need to be very sure that your customers aren't going outside just because they've tried your product and decided it wasn't good enough. We'll ask some fairly pointed questions about this in just a little while.

Customers' Third Choice

The third choice open to your customers when considering training for their staff is simply to do without. This may be because a manager has no staff turnover at all in his or her department and genuinely believes that no change is going to affect them and that there is no room to improve. In your organization, only you can say whether that belief is accurate.

But it may be the manager has neither the freedom nor the budget to go outside. He or she finds in-house training so irrelevant as to be worse than nothing.

What your customers do when buying their training will give you some information about what ought to be included in your strategy — but it won't tell you the whole story.

For example, it is possible to imagine a situation where all managers use all your product exclusively, but only because of a board directive. If the constraints are removed, what will these managers do? And where will that leave you?

Part of the plan for your strategy must be to find out what your customers really think of the training function.

Assignment:

Ask yourself the following questions and keep a record of your answers. You'll see we move into fairly confidential areas here, so you should have somewhere secure to keep your answers.

- *Which managers make the most of your training?*

- *Are they the respected go-getters or the uncritical also-rans?*

- *Do you know how many people should receive training in particular topics each year?*

- *Can you calculate how many are actually trained in each topic in-house?*

- *What does this say about the perceived quality of the training in each topic?*

- *How much of this does **not** come under the heading of technical training, management education or re-motivation?*

- *What conclusions can you draw from the pattern? Have you any potential customers who use no source of training at all? Is this because they think none is needed? Or because they see your training as worse than nothing?*

- *Are they right?*

Raising the Standing of the Training Function

We'll assume that your answers to those questions have shown areas where you'd like to improve. Here are a few ways you could encourage your customers to think better of the training function.

1. Provide Training that Meets Their Needs

Here, we'd suggest you involve managers in a regular, perhaps yearly analysis of training needs. You may feel this is something that training should do — after all you're the specialists — but remember that line management are much closer to the reality than you can ever be. Furthermore, you want them to be committed to training. Asking a lot of questions and responding positively to the answers will boost this commitment no end.

You might also consider the form your training takes. Are all courses one week long and residential? Do they have to be? If you have part-time staff with family commitments, could training be broken down into one-day modules, run locally? How about using different training methods? Would management coaching be a better match to people's needs? Or open learning? Or computer-based training?

2. Encourage Participation

If you hear managers saying 'Training? We leave all that to the training function', then training in your organization is not being effective. You need your customer's participation in many ways.

Can you think of three ways in which your customers — not your end-users, but your customers who pay for the training out of their budget — can actively participate in the training process?

Write your ideas briefly here.

-

-

-

There are many ways in which they can and **should** participate. Here are three common examples from our experience.

It is essential for managers to brief and debrief people before and after training. If training is seen as irrelevant, it may be that trainees are not being told why they are being trained and what to expect.

It is essential for managers to do some training themselves. In-house training cannot possibly deal with every aspect of every part of the organization. The training function should make support material available to managers, but must not try to do the whole job itself.

It is desirable for managers to involve themselves in the production of training:

- short-term and longer-term secondments
- working on a course on a one-off basis
- lending topic expertise
- contributing as a development tester to open learning.

All serve the dual purpose of making the material up-to-date and relevant and promoting line management's feeling of ownership.

3. Inform, Inform, Inform

'Don't tell me about your problems. I've got enough of my own.' Whether as human beings, family members, or managers or staff, we are all far more concerned with ourselves than with anyone else. As trainers, therefore, we must recognize the need to tell people about the service we offer as frequently and memorably as we can.

Your customers need to know what training is available, how to get it, what it involves, how it works, its benefits to them and what they need to do for it. At the very least, you should provide regular and up-to-date answers to these questions, ideally, in as glossy and eye-catching a form as possible. A training guide is a piece of advertising. Treat it as one. Think of some of the other tools of marketing — mailshots, exhibitions, travelling roadshows, product updates. If training can bring some fun and excitement into your customers' lives, they will love you for it.

Consumers

We're using this term to describe the people who actually receive the training. You may call them end-users, trainees, students, learners, course members, even 'punters'. They come because they're sent, by and large. Some come willingly and expectantly. Others would much rather be doing something, anything else. So how can we find out their perceptions of training? Well, by asking them, really. After all, trainees are people too. You should be asking questions, and just listening, whenever you are out and about in the organization.

List in the space below four questions which you would ask your consumers to gain information useful for your strategy.

Here are some of the questions we've used to good effect in the organizations we have worked with:

- what was the last bit of training you received?
- what did you like about it?
- what did you dislike about it?
- did it help you in your job?
- what improvements could be made?
- would you recommend it to others?
- why? Why not?

No, the questions aren't specific. The answers will cover anything from the quality of the food to the fact that the picture was out of focus. But it would be a fatal mistake to try to limit your questions just to the training. People respond to an overall experience. Below we've listed the factors we think you should try to get right, in order to gain a favourable perception of training from its consumers.

Assignment:

Select a cross-section of consumers who have had some training throughout your training function over the past two years. (The numbers involved will depend on the size of your organization and the thoroughness you require of the research.)

Ask them the questions we suggested above, and record their answers.

The results of that assignment will indicate to you the vast range of things which people will be expecting you to get right. Your end-users are looking to your people to provide amongst other things:

- a suitable environment for training
- suitable equipment
- effective tutors

- food and refreshments
- accommodation (if training is off-site)
- management support
- quality materials
- quality course design
- relevance
- briefing notes and joining instructions
- debriefing, evaluation and feedback.

Your training strategy must encompass these expectations or it will fail to achieve its full impact.

Summary

In Chapter 2 you have seen that your training function has:

- sponsors
- customers
- consumers.

You saw that each of these groups of people has different needs and expectations of the training function.

You also saw ways of identifying the needs and expectations of the different groups and learnt why it is important:

- not only to address these needs and expectations in your strategy

  but also
- to be seen to be addressing these needs.

An effective training strategy will always allow the training function

- to identify needs
- to address them
- to communicate to everyone what it's doing.

Chapter 3

Types of Organization

We're going to use this section to help you explore some of the underlying beliefs, attitudes and philosophies in your organization and to draw out their implications for your training strategy.

By the time you have read this chapter, you will be able to:

- identify your own organization with a recognized type
- identify who it is in your organization that you need to influence as a priority
- plan a strategy which will develop the positive aspects of your organization while, at the same time, countering the negative aspects of it.

During your next coffee, tea or meal break, ask the people around you the question 'What sort of organization would you say this is?' Note their answers here.

People said our organization is:

An informal chat during a tea-break does not amount to an in-depth attitude survey — but it's not an in-depth survey that you need at the moment. It's people's first reactions which give you the best clue as to what sort of organization you're actually in.

In our experience of asking this question, people's responses have generally fallen into five categories:

- 'people' answers
- 'associative' answers
- 'structural' answers
- 'historical' answers
- 'negative' answers.

If some of those terms are unfamiliar to you, don't worry. We're going to explain them one at a time so that you can match your analysis to one or more of our categories and take appropriate training measures.

1. 'People' Answers

If the people you asked said something like this:

- 'It's a very caring company'
- 'They really look after you, here'
- 'The managers are really friendly'
- 'It's a **nice** organization'

. . . then you're in a **people-oriented** environment.

How can you turn knowledge of that fact to your advantage as a trainer when planning your strategy? Write down two brief ideas in the space below.

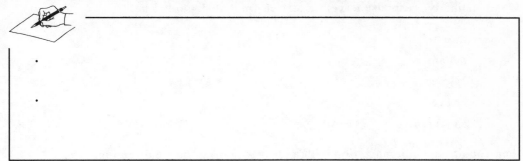

·

·

You can assume that a genuine concern for the welfare of its staff will mean that your organization will be predisposed to put training fairly high on its agenda. Consequently, you will be able to predict:

· how senior managers will react to any proposals you may make for the allocation of resources to the training function

· a fairly high level of support if you suggest developing training materials in the softer, people-oriented disciplines.

Case Study

One people-oriented organization which we have worked with encouraged its training function to set up a gymnasium for its employees' use. When the same training function suggested that employers would benefit from a course in:

· how to bank their money

· how to choose appropriate banking services

· different methods of money management

the board of directors was only too pleased to agree. Not only did this initiative prove directly beneficial to the employees, and further reinforce the image of the caring employer (with all the benefits such a reputation brings), the board was also able to introduce the idea of payment by cheque instead of in cash, and this reduced security worries and made financial controls easier.

2. 'Associative' Answers

If the instinctive response to your questions included words like:

- thrusting
- dynamic
- aggressive

  or even

- cut-throat,

then you are in an organization with a clear idea of its future direction. The organization may feel no great concern about treading on people to get there.

As a trainer you will need to consider what features your training provision must have if it is to earn the respect of the organization and its people.

In an 'aggressive' organization, what features would your training have? Take two minutes or so and write your main ideas in this space.

Our experience is that in 'aggressive' organizations, the training function does best if its strategy focuses on:

- making an obvious and speedy contribution to the achievement of the organization's financial, operational and marketing objectives

- measuring performance improvement.

People-orientation Versus Market-orientation

Trainers in either of the situations we've described so far may be tempted to indulge in value judgements. They may feel called to change the culture of the organization that they are in, and attempt to use the training function to do so.

We advise against it. Pragmatism is the best course of action in the first instance. You may be called on as an agent of change — but only when your credibility is well established.

3.   'Structural' Answers

It is possible that people answered your questions using words like:

- rigid
- hierarchical
- status-conscious
- grade-fixated.

In our experience, answers like these indicate the sort of organization where you would do well to observe the formalities which will undoubtedly be there as you prepare your strategy.

You may well notice:

- training will be expected to be formal
- your options when it comes to selecting and promoting specific training methods may be limited.

Trainers can be prone to frustration in such organizations, and frustration turns to the urge to attack the hierachical structure by introducing anarchical training— for example having the office junior giving instructions to the managing director in a tent in the woods.

The effect of such revolutionary change is almost always the same:

- **stage one** everybody hates the experience
- **stage two** their prejudice about the benefits of a rigid hierarchy are reinforced
- **stage three** change, when it comes, is delayed.

You can influence things only from a position of authority and credibility. Your long-term strategy may envisage change, but your short-term strategy for the next year or so must follow the structure that exists already. There are, after all, sound reasons why people with different levels of experience and responsibility should be trained in different things, in different ways.

4. 'Historical' Answers

You may gather that your organization is 'historical' if people answer your questions with words like:

- traditional
- old-fashioned
- fuddy-duddy
- out of the ark.

There will often be other indications of an 'historical' organization:

- · their dress
- · their attitudes to others
- · their use of surnames and initials.

Sometimes there is simply a comforting feeling of permanence.

Imagine yourself in an 'historical' situation. The organization has resisted many innovations, preferring to rely on tried and trusted ways of getting things done. You see, however, as a new trainer, that change is needed urgently, before new and hungrier competitors make devastating inroads into your customer base. Do you:

a. **institute new and exhilarating training courses in four or five of the key areas where competition is keenest?**

b. **continue with current training practice until you've 'established yourself'?**

c. **other (please specify).**

Use the space below for your answer.

(a) and (b) may be your only options — depending on just how 'historical' the organization is and how keen the competition is — but they are both fraught with danger:

(a) the sudden change may upset and antagonize so many people that it fails

(b) the slow change may be too slow. The competition will force you down.

Of the infinite possibilities under (c) we recommend one very strongly. This is a two-stage approach:

- **stage one**   spend time **explaining why** a radical overhaul is necessary
- **stage two**   when you've prepared them for the shock, go for the rapid change with complete conviction and dedication.

5.   'Negative' Answers

So far, we've looked at responses which can loosely be called descriptive. They are an attempt to convey 'the way things are round here'. Just occasionally, though, the answers you get will be judgmental:

- 'Don't know what they're doing most of the time'
- 'Lousy organization, that's what sort it is'
- 'Couldn't organize a knees-up in a brewery'.

Comments like these are as valuable as the other categories of response we've considered. But you start off by having to make a fundamental decision.

Explain in your own terms the decision you feel you would have to make in the above situation.

The decision is:

* to stay or not to stay.

Either you recognize that your **personal** objectives would be better served by reading the job advertisements regularly, **or** you accept that training has a fundamental task to do in putting right the things which have led to the attitudes. If it is not practical to put them right, or the senior management won't let you, your strategy for training can do no more than stick plasters on a terminal case of gangrene. Only you will know if that will give you job satisfaction.

Summary

In Chapter 3, you saw that whatever training strategy you devise will have to take account of the culture of the organization in which you find yourself.

In a people-oriented organization you can expect support for training — including support for introducing soft, people-orientated initiatives.

In a market-oriented, aggressive organization your contribution will need to be speedy, effective and measurable.

In a hierarchical organization you can expect training to be formal, and you must remember not to try to use a training initiative to break down the hierarchy. Training can, however, support an initiative from the organization to change the structure.

In a historical organization you should canvas support for change before trying to change things too quickly.

If negative feelings are prevalent, you must decide what contribution you can make, if any. You will need a high level of management support to achieve anything.

Assignment:

Select a group of people — between six and ten individuals will do in every case — to represent the key areas of your organization. Depending on which areas are key, they can come from:

- *different levels of the hierarchy*
- *different functions*
- *different processes.*

Ask them how they perceive the organization.

If everyone perceives the organization the same way, fine. You know what to do.

If different groups perceive the organization differently, then your ultimate strategy must stress the need to sell different benefits to different people. For example, production workers may want to hear quality-of-life benefits; board members may prefer to hear how new, ambitious targets may be reached.

Training Methodology

An important part of every trainer's job is to know what he or she will do to ensure their own professional development as trainers.

While we are keen advocates of line-managers (and other people) getting involved in training, it will nevertheless always be important for one person to have overall responsibility for training. The justification for this is partly to do with administration. After all, someone needs to be there to set up a strategy and ensure that it then runs smoothly. But it is an important part of the trainer's role to be aware of what is going on outside in the world of trainers. Information gleaned from outside the organization may impact on its internal training strategy.

This section will explore a number of things you can do to keep up-to-date with what's around and some other things you can do to assess what's going to be relevant and acceptable inside your organization.

Available Methods

Whether you take them or not, what steps could you take to find out what's happening in the outside world of training? Make your list under two headings, 'Impersonal' and 'Personal' and spend a couple of minutes writing them in the box overleaf. 'Personal', as the term implies, involves people you could contact, while 'Impersonal' will cover other avenues to explore.

The kinds of steps I could take to find out what's happening in the outside world of training are (think of three ideas for each heading below).

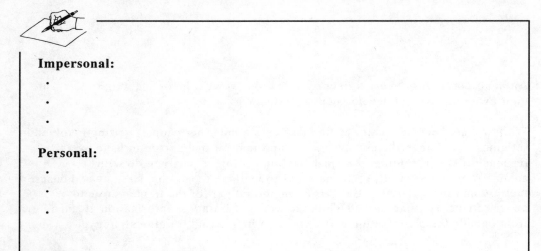

Impersonal:

-
-
-

Personal:

-
-
-

Impersonal Steps

We'll take the impersonal steps first, because they represent what is in some ways the more obvious and straightforward of our two categories.

It's to do with:

- reading the journals
- attending the exhibitions
- belonging to the professional bodies
- finding a trainers' group for your industry
- putting yourself on the Department of Employment mailing list.

It's likely that as the trainer or training manager of your organization you will be receiving mail-shots on a regular basis from all sorts of professional bodies encouraging you to apply for membership. Similarly, conference and exhibition organizers are keen to advertise their events, and you are unlikely never to have received any communication from these people.

As a plan of campaign for a new trainer, we recommend a good look through your predecessor's files to see who has been trying to woo him or her.

If you're a newly created trainer, check with your personnel department. Mail which smacks of training is often routed to personnel in the absence of a more specific job-holder.

If you are still at a loss for steps to take, contact the Business Studies department at your local university. They will have a complete list of likely publications for you to try, and reading these will give you the start you need.

Personal Steps

This category is all to do, quite unashamedly, with building contacts with people who will be willing to share information with you. It's important to remember, though, that this kind of approach needs to be two-way. If you're not prepared to give information, don't expect others to let you take it from them.

Assuming you're willing to share in this way, what contacts can you develop in:

- Chamber of Commerce?
- Lions, Rotary Club or similar charities?
- local branches of IPM, or ITD, etc?
- colleges of higher education and further education?
- universities and business schools?
- industry groups?

Assignment:

Create, if you haven't done so already, a database which can accept:

- *the names of people who contact you for help and who you contact for help*

- *the relevant addresses and phone numbers*

- *a brief description of the information requested and/or given*

- *the date of the transaction.*

It then becomes a simple task to transfer information from your letters file or your telephone message pad on to the database at regular intervals.

Before long, you will have an extensive list of people to draw on if you should need to.

Remember that the more you help people, the more they are likely to help you.

You may well have had other ideas to add to our lists. There are three important things to remember:

- no organization can prosper in a vacuum. You need this external information to help training develop and grow

- at the moment, it can only tell you what other people are doing

- you will need to decide what's applicable to you.

Let's develop that final point now.

Acceptable Methods

By this stage you will have assembled a significant body of information about training methodology, both in use and under development. You may know, for example, that one of your competitors has launched a CBT initiative to allow staff at all levels to deal direct with certain common customer queries. And that another is running a series of workshops to achieve the same end. And that you . . . well, you're in danger of being left behind because your junior staff pass all customer business on to their managers to decide what to do with it.

You have to do something — but what?

In the space below, write down three or four criteria which you believe would help you decide what to do.

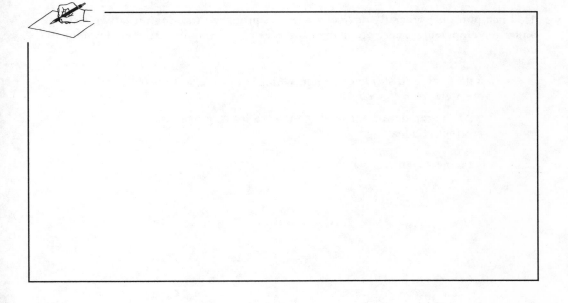

The criteria we have found successful are as follows:

- if you decide to follow your competitors' lead, the organizations where the new training method is being used must be comparable with your own in terms of size, structure, training resources, culture and outlook

- you must have the authority to introduce those things (people, equipment, procedures) which other organizations tell you are necessary for the new method to succeed

- the new method must fit with your **type of organization** as defined in Chapter 3 of this book

- you must be sure:

  a) that it will eventually work

  b) that you can predict the final form it will take.

This last point is especially critical where the proposed training initiative is still under development. There are many examples of training departments burdened down:

- with having to store equipment which was never fully used and is obsolete

- with the reputation for having blown a lot of money on an ineffective idea.

Caution is the new trainer's watchword.

Summary

In Chapter 4, you saw that the trainer's job is largely justified in terms of his or her looking outside the organization to see what is new in the world of training with a view to implementing new ideas within the organization.

The first stage was to identify sources of information which you can tap into:

- impersonal sources, such as books, magazines, exhibitions, etc
- personal sources, such as people with whom you may exchange ideas and information.

The second stage — once you had informed yourself of what was available — was to decide what was appropriate, bearing in mind your criteria:

- are your proposed methodologies being used successfully by other, senior organizations?
- have you the authority to acquire the people, equipment, etc which your methodology requires?
- does it suit your type of organization?
- will it work?

Objectives and Priorities

Trainers are always under pressure to do things: run courses, analyse problems, evaluate situations . . . and given only finite resources, inevitably these questions arise:

- what to do
- when to do it
- which task to do first.

This chapter of the book will allow you to:

- draw up a list of objectives
- place those objectives in priority order
- justify and defend your objectives and priorities.

It would be a good idea to start with an analysis of the pressures you are under at the moment. Take a few minutes and write in the box below the things you really need to do in the next couple of years if the training function is to realize its potential.

One point before you start: don't be too selective, for example, saying to yourself 'Well, we really need to achieve x, y and z but it's impossible, so I'll miss it out'.

Just put down everything you need to achieve. Broad headings will suffice at this stage, but if you would like to write a detailed list, fine; carry on on a separate piece of paper.

Trainers we asked felt under pressure to demonstrate success in the following areas:

- fundamental training
- training for change
- raising the profile of training
- personal development.

It's likely that your list of criteria for success coincides quite strangely with ours, although you may have used slightly different words and been a good deal more specific.

Look at each heading in turn.

1. Fundamental Training

This is the training which your organization cannot do without. In the first book in this series, *Understanding the Training Function,* we talked about information gathering as a key aspect of managing training. We'll assume that by a combination of listening, asking questions, reading and 'feeling the pulse' of the organization, you know as much about what's going on as anyone else — and more than most. How, then, can you use this information to help set objectives and priorities?

We don't know your organization, so we can't say what 'fundamental training' would be in your case. But in a retail company, for example, it would be in-store training for sales staff. These staff change very rapidly, but unless they have a basic product knowledge and can use a cash register, nothing gets sold. True, this is an extreme example. But we know of a large retailer whose point-of-sales training was neglected for six months. This translated very quickly into queues at the check-outs in inner-city stores where staff turnover was highest, and the customers voted with their feet and began to leave.

The point is that even a low percentage of under-trained people in a key area can have a detrimental effect on the bottom line.

In a heavy manufacturing industry, fundamental training might be for apprentices. It is simply not possible to hire experienced competent people of this kind off the street. Without effective apprentice training, nothing will be built.

Moreover, as we've already pointed out, if this fundamental, or bedrock, training is not being done properly, you are unlikely to get clearance to do anything more fancy. If your organization tells you it's satisfied with this fundamental training, a key objective must be to maintain the quality. If on the other hand, it's complaining, then putting it right must be treated as a priority.

What is 'fundamental training' in your organization?

Is it well-regarded?	Yes ☐	No ☐
Or do people complain?	Yes ☐	No ☐

If answers indicate that your fundamental training is sound, then your list of objectives which you will build into your strategy must include some way of maintaining the situation.

If, on the other hand, there are problems with your fundamental training, then it will be a priority to put those problems right. Subsequent objectives may never be met if you fail with your basics.

2.   Training for Change

Case Study

A well-known manufacturing company bought out a smaller competitor with the intention of combining both the sales forces and the product ranges. From the date of the takeover, all the salesmen would sell all the products. The trouble was, nobody told the training department.

What do you think happened? Exercise your imagination a little and write down a few thoughts in this box.

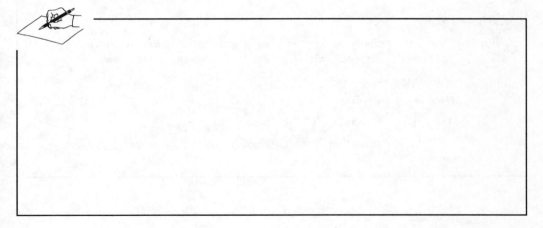

As a result, for six months head office was overwhelmed by complaints, amendments and cancellations as salesmen sold the wrong products for the wrong uses in the wrong quantities at the wrong prices. It took the company almost a year to recover from a disaster which could have been avoided by a decent programme of communication and training.

We are not suggesting that every change needs to be given top priority in your list of objectives. Some changes have more profound implications for the whole of the organization than others, and we recommend that you measure changes against the following criteria to measure their importance and their priority ranking:

- Do large numbers of people need new knowledge, skills or attitudes?

- Do any key personnel need new knowledge, skills or attitude — even though the numbers of individuals involved may be small?

- Are the consequences of those people not receiving training to face the challenge of change likely to endanger the prosperity or survival of the business?

Assignment:

Find out from the decision-makers in your organization what new initiatives are being planned. For each initiative ask the following questions:

- *Is training input required?*

- *How many people are involved?*

- *Are key people involved?*

- *Will the organization be threatened if there is no training for the change?*

Before we move on from this area, there's an important point to develop. In the case study on page 59 we said 'nobody told the training department'. The organization in question prided itself on its communications, and this was a real slip-up.

Your organization may be different, however. Depending on your situation, it could well be incumbent on you as a trainer to find out which initiatives for change are in place. If the training function has no history of making a strategic contribution, the powers that be might well not volunteer the information to the training function until it is too late for you to effect any plans.

Only you can judge whether you need to inquire about planned changes. If so, you must be ready to meet some resistance:

- Why do you need to know?
- What will you do with the information?

We advise you to be ready with your explanations.

3. Raising the Profile of Training

Certain trainers find it a very high priority indeed to raise the profile of training because they are on such a low base that key players in the organization tend to overlook them. Training might as well not be there for all the notice people take of it.

A good way to raise the profile of training is to demonstrate sound, effective training in practice. When managers start to notice their staff working better and more effectively through your efforts, then the word will start to get round.

But — there's always a but — good training is often invisible. The managers may not know it's you who has allowed success to be achieved, because you carried out your task with the minimum of disruption.

And you may not get the funds or support you need to implement your good training if no one knows you're there, and no one knows what you can do, or why they should invest in you.

It's sometimes important to undertake activities which don't impact on the bottom line at all in order to get noticed.

What activities would you undertake to raise the profile of training and enhance its reputation? List three here.

-
-
-

Trainers we know have:

- arranged 'open days'
- arranged tours for local schools
- lined up work experience sessions for local youngsters
- organized offender rehabilitation with a local prison.

These all served to boost their organization's reputation for being socially aware and responsible.

Assignment:

First, brainstorm with your team a number of 'high profile' initiatives, and select two or three of the most likely.

Then talk informally to some of the key people in your organization and see how they react to what you've come up with.

Personal Development

Some trainers are themselves short of some of the skills they need to do their jobs to the best of their ability, and for these it must be a priority as important as any other to 'plug the gap'. Otherwise, the whole training function is likely to under-perform, with serious consequences for any other objectives it has set itself.

Other trainers are able to take a longer-term view, and feel that they will need to acquire skills and experiences in the future if they are to remain at the leading edge of their profession. We believe that training is a career, and that all trainers should have an eye to their future development.

**The South East Essex
College of Arts & Technology**
Carnarvon Road, Southend-on-Sea, Essex SS2 6LS
Phone 0702 220400 Fax 0702 432320 Minicom 0702 220642

63

The following activity is the first stage in drawing up a personal career strategy.

What do you want to be doing:

> •   **in ten years' time?**

> •   **in five years' time?**

What knowledge, experience and reputation will you need to achieve these objectives?

What actions can you take in your present job to help gain the knowledge, experience and reputation you have just listed?

Which of these actions is your most urgent priority?

It is likely that your current skill-gaps loom large as urgent priorities. For example, if you see yourself as a future administrator of a large training force with a technology-based-training section, and yet you are unfamiliar with even commonplace technologies yourself, then familiarizing yourself with them is a prerequisite to progressing through your plan.

Everybody's plan is different, but there is always a logical progression throught it. The nature of the progression may depend on individual or organizational constraints and requirements.

Of course, it will now be up to you to weigh up the need for fundamental training, the need to support new initiatives, ways to raise the profile of training and your own personal development in order to achieve a balance acceptable to yourself and your organization. But we believe that a balanced set of training objectives and priorities will take account of all these elements.

Thus far in this chapter you have seen the four broad areas in which you are likely to find your objectives for your training strategy, namely:

- on-going training
- training for change
- raising the profile of the training department
- your personal development.

In each area you've seen how certain items present themselves as **priority** objectives.

- in on-going training, there will be some elements which the organization just can't do without; the alternative is failure
- in training for change, some changes involve so many people or such key people that it would be disastrous to fail to train them
- in the training department, there may be a need to raise the profile and increase credibility. Otherwise the department may not attract the funding it needs to do its job properly, and that will affect the whole organization severely
- in personal development, there is a logical progression to be pursued.

In each area, you've seen that other items are less urgent, although they are still important.

Now the time has come to identify all the objectives and rank them in priority order so that you know what you need to achieve and when, taking into account limited resources.

Strategy Grid

Over the next few pages we will show you how to design and complete a strategy grid.

Completing this grid will serve three purposes:

- it will allow you to formulate your priorities
- it will help you communicate your priorities clearly and unambiguously to any interested parties
- it will serve as the basis of a strategy monitoring system.

You will need a large sheet of plain or squared paper (A4 is the minimum size) for the grid itself, and a notepad for your workings-out.

Overview of the Grid

The outline of the grid will look like this:

	Priority Objective (3)	Priority Objective (6)	Priority Objective (9)
Area 1			
Area 2			
Area 3			
Area 4			

Clearly there is too little space to work in there, so we'll expand things to give you a better view.

The Areas

Areas 1, 2, 3 and 4 relate to:

- on-going training
- training for change
- raising the profile of the training function
- your personal development

as discussed in the earlier part of the chapter.

The Objectives

There are three columns of objectives, and each column relates to a time scale. For the purposes of this book, we're using 3, 6 and 9 months to represent short, medium and long term, but different time scales might be appropriate for you.

The Priorities

The grid is constructed so that after each objective you can enter simply L for low or H for high, depending on your assessment of the situation. Details of how to fine-tune these priorities appear on page 69.

On the next page you'll see a section of a strategy grid completed.

On-going Training

Objective (3 months)	Priority
Induction (production)	L
Induction (admin survey)	H
New software (production trial)	H
Clerical systems	L
Management skills analysis	H
Marketing skills	L
Total quality initiative (presentation)	H

As we indicated earlier, the difference between L and H is this:

- L is low priority, because it's ticking over nicely
- H is high priority, because it's failing to deliver and is damaging the organization and the reputation of the training function.

It happens that in our example there is a mixture of low and high priority items in the short term in this area.

Over the whole grid there may be areas where there are fewer objectives of lower priority. Only when the whole grid is complete will you be able to see:

- in which areas
- over what timescales

your low and high priorities lie.

> *Assignment:*
> *Draw up and complete a strategy grid for your organization.*

Monitoring the Strategy Grid

To make best use of the grid, you will need:

- to fine tune your priorities
- to check as and when objectives are met.

The same tool will allow you to carry out both these tasks.

Fine Tuning

In our example on page 68, there were four high priority tasks. We'll letter them A, B, C, D — thus:

- Induction (admin) survey   A
- New software (production) trial   B
- Management skills analysis   C
- Total quality initiative presentation   D

Starting with A and B, the fine tuning process compares the objectives two at a time. Of A and B, B is deemed more important and is moved onto the 'next round'. A is temporarily discarded.

Then, B and C are compared. B is deemed more important and C is discarded.

Finally, B and D are compared and this time D wins out. B is discarded.

D — the total quality initiative — appears to be priority one.

To find priority two, the three discards are compared in pairs; and so on until the sequence is complete.

Comparison involves asking questions such as:

- Is there a logical sequence involved?
- How many people are involved?
- What are the consequences of doing it or failing to do it?
- Is it realistic in view of the strengths of the people within the organization?

Here's a diagram to show the whole of our worked example:

Objectives

Stage 1 — Top Priority		
Objectives Compared	Objectives Selected	Priority
A/B B/C B/D	B B D	**D**
Stage 2 — Second Priority		
Objectives Compared	Objectives Selected	Priority
A/B B/C	B B	**B**
Stage 3 - Third Priority		
Objectives Compared	Objectives Selected	Priority
A/C	C	**C**
Stage 4 — Last Priority		
Objectives Compared	Objectives Selected	Priority
A	A	**A**

Checking-off Objectives

The next stage is to write down the prioritized objectives in a list and to key-in some monitoring criteria.

What criteria would you include in such a system? Write two or three in this box.

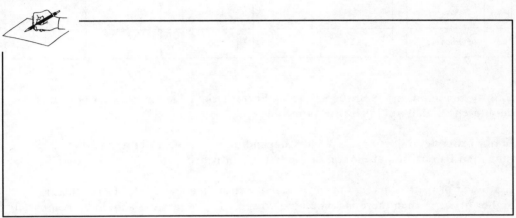

In our experience, the following monitoring criteria have been essential:

- person or team responsible
- planned and actual start dates
- planned and actual finish dates
- result
- next steps.

You will find a form like this useful, although of course you will need to adapt it for your specific purposes.

	Objective	Who	Planned start	Actual start	Planned Finish	Actual Finish	Result	Next Steps
1	TQI presentation	K.P.	1.4	1.4	22.4	22.4	Increased funds	Analyse resource needs
2	Software trial	B.M.	29.4		29.5			
3	Skills analysis		29.4		14.5			
4	Induction survey		3.5		31.5			

This system monitors your objectives and priorities in such a way that you can double-check that your priorities are right.

In our example, objectives 2, 3 and 4 depend on objective 1 being completed on time, and its position at the top of the list is confirmed.

If a lower priority objective needs an earlier start date and a later finish than a higher priority, then there is something wrong. The objectives should be compared again.

The strategy grid as we've proposed it here — and practised it ourselves — ties in closely with the principles of performance management and project management.

Performance Management

As a trainer you find out the objectives you need by reference to the company mission and the shorter-term company aims.

The objectives you find there will guide you on to what you need to do and when — and your monitoring of those objectives will allow you to feed information back up the system which will be essential when senior managers and the board come to review the aims and the mission at the prescribed intervals.

Project Management

Each objective becomes a project in its own right, with start and end dates determined, and ultimately resources and budget allocated to it.

As a trainer you can run these projects yourself or (perhaps more appropriately in larger organizations) you can break each one down into smaller sub-projects and delegate their completion to other members of your team.

Explaining and Defending Your Strategy

In front of whom might you be called to explain and defend your strategy? Write some names and titles in the box below.

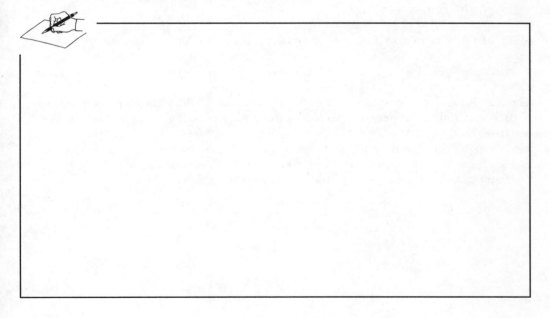

Trainers we've known have been asked testing questions by:

- senior managers
- board members
- colleagues
- their team members
- juniors
- trainees.

In fact, everyone who has a vested interest in the success of the training function can reasonably be expected to know:

- what you're doing
- what you hope to achieve
- when you're doing it and, justifiably,
- **why** you're doing it.

Many of the queries you'll be able to answer on the spot as you become familiar with the task you're undertaking, but your strategy monitoring system is potentially so compact that you'll be able to carry it round with you.

Then, as long as you keep the grid regularly updated — the **next steps** entry is particularly important here — you'll be able to answer all queries confidently and consistently. And so will your team. There is an expression which extols the virtues of 'all singing from the same hymn-sheet' — in other words, delivering a consistent message. A written source document is invaluable as an aid for consistency of message, and the strategy monitoring grid fits the bill exactly.

Summary

Chapter 5 of this book explored first of all the areas where you are likely to find your objectives for the training function:

- on-going training
- training for change
- raising the profile of the training function.

Then it analysed, in each of those areas, some of the criteria which will enable you to decide whether the objectives are high or low priority.

You then moved on to examine a method of fine-tuning and monitoring your objectives over the short, medium and longer term. By a process of comparison you sorted out all the objectives into priority order.

Then you saw how to apply criteria to each objective — criteria you can use to measure each objective to see whether it has been achieved or not; in short — a monitoring system.

You saw how the completed strategy monitoring system fits in smoothly with the idea of performance management and project management.

Lastly, you saw how the monitoring system allows you to explain and defend your strategy.

Assignment:

Prepare a strategy monitoring system for your organization, focusing on short-, medium- and long-term objectives.

*Make a note of **who** looks at your strategy grid, and **what for**. Is it of greater use to you as an organizing and administering tool, or as a planner and on-going discussion document?*

Chapter 6

Strategies and Resources

This is the final chapter in this book, and it is designed to help you to formalize your training not only so it is effective, but also so that it maximizes the use made of resources within your organization.

By the time you've completed this chapter, you will be able to:

- explain the purpose of a training policy statement
- state what should be on it
- describe the characteristics of effective trainers
- outline major resourcing issues which affect you.

Training Policy Statement

If you're reading this book, it is likely that you're a policy-maker. That, by definition, involves you in establishing strategies and the first strategy we would recommend is to create a training policy statement. Even if you already have one, you should question whether you are happy with it.

Carry out the following activity based on:

- your organization's existing statement
- a combination of what you like and don't like about it
- what you would like to see included in a statement (if only it existed).

In your opinion what are the principal factors which should be addressed in a training policy statement? Think of three principal factors and list them below.

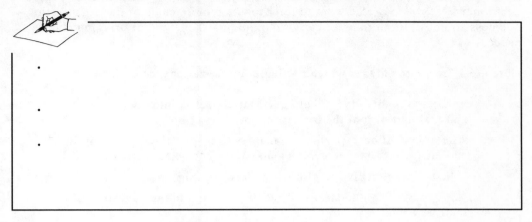

We thought the following factors should be addressed:

Who Should Receive Training?

The obvious answer is 'everybody'. But obvious answers are not always the right ones. You might want the policy statement to refer to:

- 'All full-time staff'
- 'All staff and management'
- 'All staff covered by a union agreement'.

Or you might want to break training down by category:

- 'All staff under 25 years of age are entitled to day-release'
- 'All staff receiving a performance review should be trained to meet needs identified in the review'
- 'All new employees will receive induction training'.

What is Training Intended to Achieve?

You'll probably want the policy statement to say that 'training is intended to improve performance'. You may also want to refer to 'the requirements of the organization's business strategy', or more practically to 'training as a method of bringing about successful change'.

Here are a few more phrases which particular organizations have included:

- 'Induction is intended to help new starters settle into the company and feel part of it at the earliest opportunity'.

- 'The organization expects its managers to be promoted from within and operates a management development scheme to facilitate this'.

- 'All staff will receive Health and Safety training'.

- 'All newly promoted staff will receive training in the key skills of their new job'.

- 'The organization believes that staff and heads of department should receive refresher and follow-up training throughout their careers'.

What is the Route into Training?

Even in quite large, sophisticated organizations, many people have no idea how they get themselves on to a training programme, so your training policy statement should tell them. There are many different approaches. The one(s) you choose are less important than ensuring that people are aware of them.

Here are some possibilities:

- 'The open learning centre is open from 09.00 to 21.00 every working day. All staff are entitled to register for an open learning course, provided it is not over-subscribed'.

- 'Immediately following the appraisal interview, recommendations should be passed to the centre, who will confirm acceptance within a month'.

- 'Details of forthcoming courses will be published twice yearly. Managers wishing to nominate should do so using the nomination forms enclosed with the course details'.

- 'Any member of staff can ask to be considered for a course or training package at any time by completing a form which is available from the personnel department'.

How Will Training be Delivered?

This looks to be a straightforward question, but it has some profound and far-reaching implications. From the viewpoint of the training policy statement, it might be worthwhile saying that:

- 'This company intends to be at the forefront of new training technology'

  or

- 'All new staff will receive off-the job induction training'

  or

- 'All training will take place at the company residential training centre'

  or

- 'This organization believes in the effectiveness of open learning'

  or

- 'Managers are responsible for training their staff'.

Don't forget, though, that drawing up a training policy statement is not an end in itself.

Should you choose to adopt any of these phrases as part of your training policy statement, you are committing yourself to a course of action and to following it through to its logical conclusion. We shall develop this idea further when we look at the activities necessary for the successful implementation of different training methods in book 6. For the moment we shall look at just one example from our list of phrases.

'All new staff will receive off-the-job induction training'. What must the training function do to ensure this happens successfully? Think of four actions if the training is done by the training department.

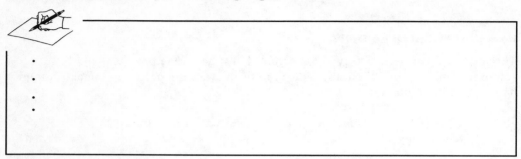

Think of four actions to be taken by the training department if the training is to be done by someone from the line.

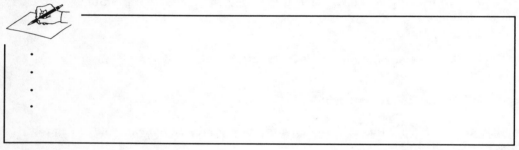

First of all, we need a decision. Will off-the-job training be conducted by someone:

·   from the training department

·   from the line?

Then there is the consideration of what happens next.

If the Training Department:

- send out joining instructions
- book training room
- allocate instructor
- book external training specialists
- copy handouts/exercises, etc
- book equipment, films, etc.

If the Line:

- ensure managers see training as their responsibility
- provide effective trainers' notes
- make support material: ensure handouts, films, etc, are available
- ensure equipment is available
- check that suitable rooms are available
- build in quality checks.

Training Plan

The mere existence of a training policy statement, however, does not itself mean that any meaningful training will actually happen. We know of a national organization with a long-established training function. Over decades the training specialists had talked to managers, carried out training needs analyses, developed programmes and published brochures. The trouble was that no one really understood precisely **what** was available, **where**, **for whom**, **when** . . . and so on.

Our reference here to a training plan is a plea for a simple, logical structure to the training provision. Just as customers don't spend much time thinking about the layout, storage space and display techniques of the shops they go to, so your customers won't have enough time in their busy working days to analyse in depth a complex and confusing training product.

What people actually want and need is something simple, preferably graphic, that will tell them at a glance what training is available for them, when, where and, with any luck, what the training will be like.

As soon as possible within the process, draw up a training matrix so that everyone in the organization gets the information they need simply, quickly and clearly.

Training as a People Business

In this section, we're going to look in some detail at the sort of people you might want in the training department and the kind of environment and atmosphere which would help to attract and retain them.

In your opinion, what sort of people make good trainers?

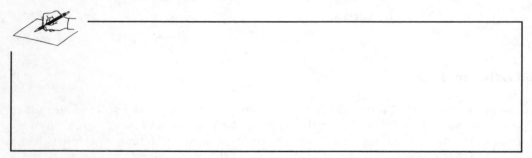

Training is a people business, whether you are a lone trainer or part of a team. As a lone trainer you might be dealing with line supervisors taking a training role, consultants and, of course, trainees.

If you are in a team, you can expect to come across professional, qualified, trainers, people who have 'evolved' into trainers, seconded managers, and so on.

In fact, the quality of staff who are eager to join the training team is a useful indicator of the training function's internal reputation.

Of course, there isn't just one answer to this question. We found it helpful to separate people's **background and experience** on the one hand from their **personalities** on the other hand.

Background and Experience

We've seen the best results from training departments when they contain both seconded and permanent staff. Seconded staff, because they know the business, can make training relevant and up-to-date. They speak from experience, which makes them convincing. But, usually, they need a while to settle into training. As much as one-third of their secondment is likely to be spent learning the job, so they are unlikely to be able to contribute much in the way of new approaches. And if part of your training is delivered through open learning or computer-based training, they may never acquire the relevant skills. That's why you need permanent staff as well. These should be experienced people from a training background who know a lot about what's happening in the internal training world and can contribute directly to the department's whole strategy. They should also have the specialist training skills — for example, authoring, design research expertise, and presentation — which seconded staff may not possess.

Personality

An ideal trainer would have the patience of Job, the creativity of Leonardo da Vinci and the leadership qualities of the Pied Piper of Hamelin. And if you found them, you couldn't afford them.

In the real world, however, you can look for analytical people who can evaluate problems, identify training needs and find solutions to them. You need creative people who can come up with new, but workable, ideas and approaches. But they must be practical enough to follow them through to make them happen. You need people who are good with people. They must be good communicators, sympathetic, easy to talk to.

Of course such qualities rarely come together. So you might divide the activities of the training function into 'backroom' and 'the acceptable face of . . . ' Only you will know your people well enough to say if this is necessary.

But however good your people are, their performance will be radically affected by the environment and atmosphere in which they are expected to work. People perform better when they are happy at work and comfortable in their surroundings. There are some very important physical considerations to take into account regarding the environment.

Preferably it will be clear, light, and relatively recently decorated. It must be a safe and healthy environment — all these things add up to minimum requirements — and we are well aware that many trainers might have to make the best of a bad job.

But there is something else, less tangible, but just as important as everything already mentioned above.

In your opinion, how should the training department 'feel' to get the best out of people? Write down two/three ideas here.

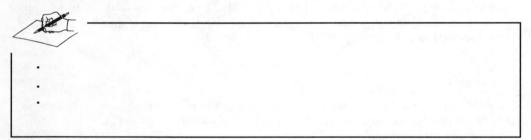

You could run an authoritarian regime and justify it on the grounds that everyone knows exactly what they should be doing all the time. The trouble is, if you run your training department like a military operation, you must be prepared to accept the down-side of that, too. Your colleagues might be committed to their duty, but you might also have rubbed out their individual flair.

Trainers are responsible for improving the performance of huge numbers of people. They need to be allowed to fail — preferably not too often. The kind of environment most likely to nurture this will maintain a status-free respect for individual qualities and expertise. That may not be easy to achieve if you operate in an otherwise hierarchical bureaucracy — but it is worth trying!

Regular Review

Some organizations include in their training policy statement a commitment to a regular review of training, to be conducted by training management and presented to members of the board. If you don't do this at the moment, we'd recommend it.

What benefits would such a review have?

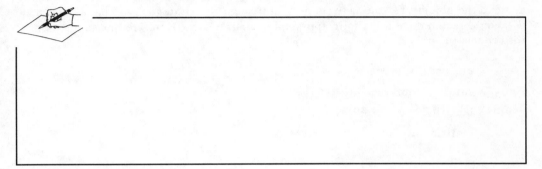

Here are the benefits we thought of:

- the training department can 'internally market' itself to the board
- there is visible commitment to training at board level, and this is clear throughout the organization
- the training department, and its product, gets tenders from the board's review
- there is increased senior management support of training
- training is seen to report to the board at a strategic level.

So, whether you write it into the training policy statement or not, we feel that a regular review at board level can do nothing but good. Of course, this should only be the visible tip of a much more detailed and extensive evaluation process, which we shall look at in book 7 of this series.

Resourcing

It is all well and good to suggest laying down strategies, providing the right environment and attracting the right people, but you cannot conjure all this out of thin air. You **can** solve some problems by throwing money and resources at them.

So, whilst we cannot advise you specifically about the resources you will need to achieve the objectives you have set and implement the strategies you have chosen, we would recommend a realistic appraisal of your needs. Here are our suggestions for criteria to apply:

- current resources
- future resources
- benefits
- realism.

Current Resources

List in the box below your four most precious current resources.

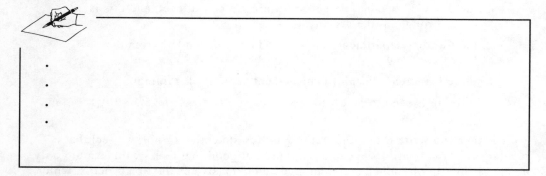

-
-
-
-

We can't say exactly what you put as your four most precious resources, but we'd be disappointed if you didn't put your people or yourself top of the list — which might look like this:

- people
- budget
- premises
- equipment

although we admit the possibility of other items, such as:

- contacts with other organizations

  or

- external suppliers.

Once you've broadly established what your resources are, then you can start to appraise them more closely. Your people (including yourself) are worth the most detailed examination. Ask yourself (or ask them if you don't know):

- what **experiences** they have had
- what **strengths** they feel they could develop
- what **ideas** they have developed
- what **relation** they have with potential sources of help or information
- what **training** and **development** they have had.

Then, when you've got a fix on exactly what your resources are, you can begin to analyse your current situation. Here are some suggestions as to questions you need answers to.

Are any resources under-used? The computer terminal which no one has used for two years and the satellite receiving equipment which is so infrequently aired that most people don't know what it is are obvious examples. These things can be incorporated in your future plans or made available for a fee or for goodwill's sake to other departments or other organizations. Or they can be scrapped to make way for newer more useful tools. But your staff can be under-used, too.

Case Study

Only when Tom Bullevant made a risqué comment in Danish during his retirement speech did his boss the training manager realize that he spoke anything other than English. It turned out that Tom spoke five languages more or less fluently —much to the chagrin of the training manager who had been telling his customers for years that the training department didn't do foreign language tuition.

Do your resources need replacement? Such is the pace of change these days that you can **feel** your equipment is up to date, but looking in catalogues may come as a shock. Don't be sentimental about old materials. 'They've worked before and they'll work again' is true: but what image are you creating? And are you efficient?

Do you need more resources? Yes, we all need more resources; the measure of our budget is the measure of our clout within the organization . . . but will the increase in resources justify itself in increased output? A 20 per cent increase in resources is not justified if it will only bring a 10 per cent increase in efficiency.

How does your productivity compare with other people's training? Productivity can be defined as output divided by input. A figure of greater than one therefore represents a gain or a benefit to the organization. Your input is easy to measure: budget, hours worked, resources on hand. But your output? This is more a qualitative than a quantitative thing and will involve some evaluation of training; evaluation is dealt with in book 7 of this series.

Are you having it easy or are you over-stretched? Either case is bad. In the former you need to take on more work, and in the latter you need to check first that all your excessive activity is indeed productive. Re-working and mistake-fixing don't count. If you are being productive and you're over-stretched, it is time for an increase in your resourcing.

Future Resources

The key to acquiring increased resources is to:

- describe the minimum you need to achieve in order to benefit the business as effectively as you can and **then**

- describe the resources you need to do that.

In other words, put the task first. Otherwise, you will sound like you're asking for as much as you can get and only then working out what you can do with it.

To focus on the resourcing implications of your future plans, what key questions do you feel you should ask? List four in this box.

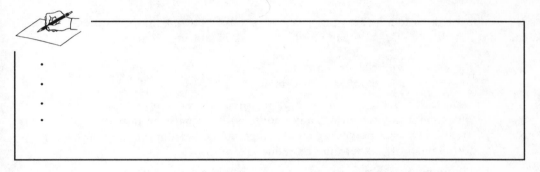

-
-
-
-

Here are our suggestions:

- what will your objectives and strategies mean in terms of cost?
  That is to say:
  — numbers of course members (don't forget down-time)
  — training packages
  — travel
  — accommodation
  — research
  — publicity

- how does this future requirement compare with your current?

- assuming acceptance of your future plans, is there a surplus of resources at present or a shortfall?

- if there's a shortfall, can you justify increased resources by comparison with industry standards of productivity? Again, evaluation raises its head here.

Benefits

Remember that in all probability you're approaching the people with the purses asking at least for the maintenance of your current level of funding, and maybe for an increase.

It's easier for them to say 'no' than 'yes'. 'Yes' implies a risk, an investment which may not pay dividends. You can reduce this risk by stating clearly:

- the way in which your request for resources relates to the organization's achievement of its mission

- what quantifiable return the organization will receive for its investment in you: how many people will be qualified in which areas? By what percentage will telephone calls from the branches to the head office helpline be reduced?

- the unquantifiable return you can offer: enhanced reputation, increased workforce co-operation and commitment, greater staff loyalty.

Realism

Any request for funding or increased resources will need to take account of ordinary, workaday realities. The economic climate, for example, will decide some people against increased funding for anything; calls for savings, economies and cost-cuttings simply dim out everything else. In circumstances like this, is it not perhaps more sensible in the longer term to play along with the realists and pragmatists rather than making enemies of them? Is it perhaps politically wiser to tone down your requests this year, with a view to increasing them next year, by which time your reputation for level-headedness will be established?

We cannot say. We have seen situations where the opposite tack has been taken to great effect. The trainer has applied for increases in the face of all received wisdom and been acclaimed as bold and far-sighted. Only you can measure your situation. We do advise you, whatever you do, to consider these questions:

- What extra resources would you need if your plans involved just 'more of the same'?
- What further resources will you need to reflect the experimental nature of new initiatives?
- Are you sure you haven't underestimated? (You won't get such a good reception if you have to go back for an unbudgeted increase.)
- Can the organization afford what you're asking for?
- If not, what can you trim?
- Is this a time of expansion, consolidation or contraction?
- What can you reasonably expect at this time?

Summary

This final chapter has brought you to the end of your planning stage. You saw that:

- if you have a training policy statement, you may need to amend it as appropriate to your strategic aims
- if you do not have a training policy statement, write one
- your statement should address:
  — who should receive the training
  — what the training intends to achieve
  — resource implications

- resourcing depends on a realistic appraisal of what you've got and what you need
- when reviewing your resourcing, you should:
  — consider you current resources
  — quantify your future resources
  — explain the benefits to the budget-holders
  — be realistic.

We wish your plan every success.

Assignment:

Taking your training policy statement, draft a document defining what resources will be required to fulfil its plans for the next year.

Include:

- *budget*
- *people*
- *hardware*
- *other materials.*

Discuss this document with the decision makers in your organization.

The South East Essex
College of Arts & Technology
Carnarvon Road, Southend-on-Sea, Essex SS2 6LS
Phone 0702 220400 Fax 0702 432320 Minicom 0702 220642